S0-AJI-457

Do Alaskans Live In Igloos?

– Show Me Your Alaska Home

A Children's Book by

Bernd and Susan Richter

To the Scotts Valley
Library
Enjoy this tour through
beautiful Alaska!

Susan Richter

Bernd Richter

Published by

Saddle Pal Creations, Cantwell, Alaska

Denali Park, Alaska, September 7, 2000

The authors wish to acknowledge the following people: Our good friends Lynne P. Beykirch, Pamela Patterson, and Nelda Osgood for their comments and editorial support; and Jenny Whittier, Development Manager at C&C Offset Printing Co., for sharing her expertise in book production.

Dedicated to family and friends in Germany, Alaska, and Outside for all their help through very difficult times.

Text and Illustration copyright ©1998 by Bernd and Susan Richter

Second Printing, May 2000

ISBN #0-9663495-2-0

All rights reserved. No portion of this book may be reproduced in any form without the publisher's written approval.

Published by Saddle Pal Creations

P.O. Box 175, Cantwell, Alaska, USA

For other titles available from Saddle Pal Creations please see last page of this book.

Printed in Hong Kong.

When I was a child, I saw a photo of a man standing next to some igloos. Do you know what an igloo is? An igloo is a hut made from blocks of hard snow.

"This is from Alaska," mom said when she saw me looking at the picture.

"What's Alaska?" I asked.

"Alaska is a state of the United States, just like California or Texas," she replied. "It is located near the North Pole and it is covered with snow and ice. That is why people there live in igloos," she explained.

"Have you been to Alaska, Mom?" I asked.

"Oh no," she replied, "it is too far away."

Ever since then, I have wondered about Alaska and its people living in igloos. So when I had the chance to visit this faraway state, I jumped at the opportunity. I would finally see this land of snow and ice, and I would sleep in an igloo!

This is the story of my search for an igloo in Alaska.

When you fly over Alaska you can see how big this state is. There are huge areas of green forests and meadows, and there are equally large areas of brown mountain ranges. There are also big areas that are covered by white snow and ice both in the winter and in the summer.

Those could be the areas where I will find the igloos, I thought as I flew toward Alaska's largest city, Anchorage.

As we approached Anchorage, I imagined how this igloo city would look. How exciting it must be to live in a city where all the buildings are made from snow. I could hardly wait to see huge office buildings, gas stations, movie theaters, super markets, churches, and even schools made from snow.

And soon I would stay at an igloo hotel. I hoped they have lots of warm blankets.

OH, WHAT A DISAPPOINTMENT!

ANCHORAGE IS MADE FROM BUILDINGS JUST
LIKE ANY OTHER BIG CITY. IT IS A NICE CITY, BUT
THE OFFICE BUILDINGS, SUPER MARKETS, GAS
STATIONS, CHURCHES, AND SCHOOLS LOOK THE
SAME AS THE ONES AT HOME.

I WALKED AROUND FOR A WHOLE DAY, BUT I COULDN'T FIND A SINGLE IGLOO.
MAYBE ALL THE IGLOOS WERE BULLDOZED TO MAKE ROOM FOR ALL THESE
MODERN BUILDINGS? IF THAT IS SO, I WONDERED, "COULD I FIND IGLOOS IF
I TRAVELED AWAY FROM THE BIG CITY?"

So I rented a car and drove out of the city. Surely I would find a small village soon. I could already imagine it -- a small town on a hillside with bright, white igloos that could be seen from far away. The people in that town wouldn't tear down igloos just to make room for office buildings.

What do you think? Will I find a small town that is made up entirely of igloos?

I GUESS NOT!

THE HOUSES IN THAT TOWN WERE STRANGE, BUT
THEY WEREN'T MADE FROM SNOW. NEVER BEFORE
HAD I SEEN HOUSES LIKE THAT. THEY WERE MADE
FROM WHOLE TREE TRUNKS, CALLED LOGS. THE LOGS
WERE STACKED ON TOP OF EACH OTHER TO MAKE
THE WALLS OF THE HOUSES. TO PREVENT THE LOGS
FROM ROLLING OFF EACH OTHER, GROOVES WERE
CARVED OUT OF THE UNDERSIDE OF EACH LOG
INTO WHICH THE UNDERLYING LOG WOULD FIT. COOL!

BUT THERE WAS SOMETHING ELSE THAT WAS STRANGE. EVERY BIG HOUSE HAD
A SMALL BUILDING BEHIND OR NEXT TO IT. AND, THERE WAS ANOTHER LITTLE
CABIN THAT WAS BUILT HIGH UP ON STILTS WITH A LARGE LADDER LEANING
AGAINST IT. COULD EVERY CHILD IN THIS TOWN HAVE A PLAY HOUSE?

I HAD TO ASK ONE OF THE OWNERS WHAT THOSE SMALLER BUILDINGS WERE.

THE ONE HIGH UP IS CALLED A **CACHE**. IT ISN'T A PLAY HOUSE AT ALL! IT IS USED TO STORE MEAT AND OTHER FOODS. IT IS BUILT HIGH UP TO KEEP WILD ANIMALS, LIKE THE GRIZZLY BEARS, FROM GETTING TO THE FOOD. THE BEARS WOULD LOVE TO EAT ALL THE FOOD THAT PEOPLE STORE FOR THE LONG WINTER.

THE OTHER BUILDING IS CALLED AN **OUTHOUSE**. IT IS CALLED AN OUTHOUSE BECAUSE YOU HAVE TO GO OUTSIDE THE HOUSE TO GO TO THE BATHROOM. YES, THE OUTHOUSE HAS A TOILET! HAVE YOU EVER USED SUCH AN OUTHOUSE? MAYBE YOU DID AT A CAMPGROUND? AS I LEARNED ON MY TRIP, MANY PEOPLE IN ALASKA USE OUTHOUSES, BECAUSE THEIR HOUSES DON'T HAVE PLUMBING. DO YOU KNOW WHAT THAT MEANS? IT MEANS THEIR HOUSES HAVE NO SHOWERS, NO SINKS, AND NO FAUCETS. DO YOU THINK YOU WOULD LIKE LIVING IN SUCH A HOUSE?

I hadn't come to Alaska to look at toilets!

So I continued on foot toward the snow-covered mountains, where I was sure to find some igloos. On the way, I came to a creek where a man was washing a skillet in the water.

"That must be a dirty skillet," I yelled to him across the creek.
"What?" he asked.
"Your skillet," I repeated, "it must be very dirty if you have to wash it for so long."
"That's not a skillet," he laughed, "it's a gold pan. And I am not washing the pan. I am washing sand and rocks looking for gold. I'm a gold miner. I live here all summer hoping to strike it rich!"

Hmm -- could he be living in an igloo? Surely, he wouldn't build a fancy log cabin for just a few summer months!

16

This time I was right and wrong. The miner doesn't live in a fancy cabin, but he also doesn't live in an igloo. Instead, he lives in a rundown cabin that must have been built a hundred years ago. It is very primitive, but it serves him very well during the four or five months he spends there every summer. Obviously, he hasn't found much gold yet, or he wouldn't live in a cabin with a leaky roof.

I wanted to ask the miner where I could possibly find an igloo, but he was so busy looking for gold that I didn't want to disturb him any further. I wished him good luck as I continued on my way, hoping I would also have good luck in my search for an igloo.

As I got closer to the snow-covered mountains, I ran into a group of mountain climbers. They were on their way to North America's highest mountain, Mt. McKinley. They carried big backpacks and even snowshoes, which helped them walk on deep snow.

"Hi guys," I greeted them. "How long will it take you to climb this huge mountain?"
"Oh, it depends on the weather," they replied. "If the weather holds, we could make it in a few days. If it starts snowing and blowing, it could take a couple of weeks."

A couple of weeks? If they stay on a snow-covered mountain for a couple of weeks, then they must be sleeping in igloos! Surely, there can't be a hotel on top of such a high mountain. What do you think?

20

I WANTED TO ASK THE CLIMBERS ABOUT THE IGLOOS,
BUT THEY HAD ALREADY LEFT TO CONTINUE THEIR
LONG HIKE UP THE MOUNTAIN.

FORTUNATELY THOUGH, I HAD BROUGHT
ALONG MY BINOCULARS. WITH THOSE, I
COULD HAVE A FIRST LOOK AT IGLOO CITY
ON MT. MCKINLEY WITHOUT HAVING TO CLIMB
THIS HUGE MOUNTAIN!

WAIT, THOSE AREN'T IGLOOS. THEY'RE TENTS! LOTS AND LOTS OF TENTS.
OF COURSE, HIKERS AND CLIMBERS ALWAYS SLEEP IN TENTS. THAT IS WHY
THEY CARRY THOSE BIG BACKPACKS.

I wondered now if I would ever find an igloo in Alaska. Where else could I look? Who could I ask? I was running out of ideas and out of time, when I happened to stumble upon a ranger station. And what luck, Park Ranger Theresa was at the station when I arrived there.

"Ranger Theresa," I said, "I am looking for an igloo. Will you tell me where I can find one?"
"Hmm," she murmured, "we don't have any igloos here at the park. We have bear dens though, which are probably the closest you will come to an igloo. Who told you that there are igloos in Alaska?" she asked.

"My mom told me," I answered, "and I have proof
of it. Look here at this picture."
I pulled the picture out of my pocket and
handed it to her.

"Oh," she said, "this is an Eskimo man. This
picture was probably taken at an area far
north from here at the coast. You should
go there if you want to find an igloo."
"Thanks so much, Ranger Theresa," I said, "you were a big help."

Finally, I had a solid lead on where to go to find igloos. So I
started my long trip north to find the Eskimo people and their igloos.

On my way north, I kept asking others where I could find Eskimo people. Do you know who the Eskimo people are?

I learned that they are some of the first people who settled in Alaska a long, long time ago. Together with the Athabascan, Tlingit, Haida, Tsimshian, and Aleut people, they are known as Alaska Natives.

I found out that I could find some of them nearby at a summer fishing camp. Such a camp is not quite like a summer camp for children. Instead, it is a camp where everybody works hard to catch fish for the winter. Maybe that is where they use igloos! Maybe igloos are not to live in but to keep fish fresh, just like a giant regrigerator! That would make sense because there is no electricity for a refrigerator at a remote fishing camp. Soon I would find out.

WHAT A DISAPPOINTMENT! AGAIN, NO IGLOOS, ONLY TENTS.

"WHERE ARE YOUR IGLOOS?", I ASKED A LADY WHO
WAS CUTTING FISH INTO THIN SLICES. "AREN'T
YOU ESKIMOS?"
"OH YES," SHE REPLIED, "WE ARE ESKIMOS OF THE
YUPIK TRIBE, BUT WE DON'T LIVE IN IGLOOS.
WHO TOLD YOU THAT WE DO?"
WHEN I SHOWED HER THE PICTURE, SHE LOOKED AT IT WITH MUCH INTEREST.
"YOU KNOW," SHE SAID, "THIS MUST BE A PICTURE FROM A CANADIAN IGLOO
VILLAGE. IN NORTHERNMOST CANADA, OUR ESKIMO RELATIVES USED TO LIVE IN
IGLOOS. BUT HERE IN ALASKA, WE NEVER LIVED IN IGLOOS BECAUSE WE ALWAYS
HAD OTHER BUILDING MATERIAL AVAILABLE. WE MAY BUILD AN IGLOO AS A
STORM SHELTER WHEN NEEDED, BUT WE LIVE IN HOUSES LIKE ANYBODY ELSE."

NOW I KNOW -- ALASKANS DON'T LIVE IN IGLOOS.
BUT THEY LIVE IN A BEAUTIFUL STATE!

Titles available from Saddle Pal Creations, P.O. Box 175, Cantwell, AK 99729, USA

When Grandma and Grandpa visited Alaska they...

ISBN # 0-9663495-0-4

How Alaska Got Its Flag

ISBN # 0-9663495-4-7

When Grandma visited Alaska she...

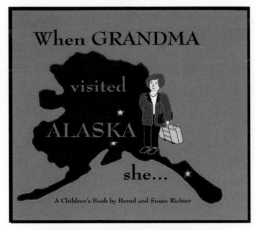

ISBN # 0-9663495-1-2

Do Alaskans Live In Igloos?

ISBN # 0-9663495-2-0

Peek-A-Boo Alaska

ISBN # 0-9663495-5-5
A lift-the-flap board book for toddlers

Uncover Alaska's Wonders

ISBN # 0-9663495-3-9
A lift-the-flap book